21 DAYS *of* PRAISE

SEEKING GOD'S FACE
INSTEAD OF HIS HAND

LUCILLE WILLIS

WESTBOW
PRESS®
A DIVISION OF THOMAS NELSON
& ZONDERVAN

The Authorized (King James) Version of the Bible ('the KJV'), the rights in which are vested in the Crown in the United Kingdom, is reproduced here by permission of the Crown's patentee, Cambridge University Press.

WestBow Press books may be ordered through booksellers or by contacting:

WestBow Press
A Division of Thomas Nelson & Zondervan
1663 Liberty Drive
Bloomington, IN 47403
www.westbowpress.com
1 (866) 928-1240

ISBN: 978-1-5127-7549-5 (sc)
ISBN: 978-1-5127-7551-8 (hc)
ISBN: 978-1-5127-7550-1 (e)

Library of Congress Control Number: 2017902225

Print information available on the last page.

WestBow Press rev. date: 03/14/2017

This book is dedicated to my mother, who always encouraged me to write, believe in myself, and pursue my dreams. Mom, you fought the good fight and finished the course. You gave everything you had, and we all are better people because of you. You are my biggest cheerleader, and although you are no longer with us, I find comfort in knowing that you still cover us and that God said to you, "Well done, my good and faithful servant."

Mom, you are deeply loved and missed. Thank you mom!

The Lord is my shepherd;
I shall not want.
He maketh me to lie down
in green pastures:
he leadeth me beside the still waters.
He restoreth my soul:
he leadeth me in the paths of righteousness
for his name's sake.
Yea, though I walk through the valley
of the shadow of death, I will fear no evil:
for thou art with me;
thy rod and thy staff they comfort me.
Thou preparest a table before me
in the presence of mine enemies:
thou anointest my head with oil;
my cup runneth over.
Surely goodness and mercy
shall follow me all the days of my life:
and I will dwell in the house of the Lord for ever.
—Psalm 23

CONTENTS

Section 5 Let the Journey Begin!

Section 6 Twenty-One Days of Praise Journal

ACKNOWLEDGMENTS

I am grateful to several people, without whom this book would have never been possible. My loving husband, Bill, you are an amazing man. When I needed your support and encouragement you were always there. With you by my side, I know that we can accomplish anything. Your love catapults me to higher levels of my true self. I am grateful that you are the man that God chose to not only love me but to also cover me. You are my love, my best friend, and my king, and I am excited to see all that God has in store for us. Our new journey has only begun!

My children, Jessica and Darius, and granddaughter, Neveah, I love you more than words can adequately express. Thank you for your support and advise. You give me hope for the future. My prayer is that God will continue to keep you and use you as vessels on the earth for His kingdom.

My sister, Tangee, you continue to be my quiet support system whenever I need a sounding board or a jolt of laughter. You have an amazing ministry of encouragement. May you walk in the calling God has placed upon your life.

Pastor Henry J and Minister Connie Healey and Pastor David and Minister Erika Walker, I am in awe of your display of love and obedience to God and your love for His people.

My husband and I continue to grow in every area of our lives under your leadership. You will always have a special place in our hearts. May your latter days be greater, and may God continue to bless you all!

My business/success coach, Dr. Stacia Pierce, you called out to my inner soul and I answered. You brought me back to the realization of who I am created to be. I will never forget sitting at your Ultimate Success Tour in Chicago and thinking, *I know this stuff, but where have I been for the past ten years, and why have I robbed myself of the life I was destined to live?* So I took action and changed my life. My goodness! How much I have accomplished in a short amount of time, including writing this book, and the best is yet to come. Much success to you and all that you put your hands to. You deserve this season of harvest because of your obedience, faithfulness, and seeds of greatness that you plant into the lives of others. Enjoy it! Let the light of God's blessing shine bright.

To my WestBow Press family, thank you for amazing support, a great product, and an opportunity of a lifetime.

Finally, to Mikey Monday, you are a creative and talented photographer. Thank you for my amazing author photograph.

INTRODUCTION

21 Days of Praise is a guide to your spiritual praise journey that will help you discover a more intimate relationship with God. It will prepare you for a lifetime of seeking His presence and continuous praise. It will help you experience twenty-one days of transformation and maximize your personal connection with God.

He wants your greatest gift: your time. Each day you will have a key Bible scripture to meditate on and ample journaling space to reflect on what He is saying to you and to shower Him with powerful words of purposeful praise.

You are not reading this book by accident. God wants you to go to the next level in Him. Do you have the courage to praise Him on purpose? If you do, I am convinced that by the end of this journey, you will have a new way of thinking, praising, speaking, writing, and living. A new you! May this journey help you to become all that He has created you to become.

I thank God for choosing me to go through this journey with you. Praising Him has delivered me from just seeking His hand to seeking His face. It has taught me to love Him, praise Him, and know Him even more. I am forever grateful for this journey and honored to be your guide. I pray my words will honor Him, bless you, and lead you to a more abundant life in Him. *21 Days of Praise* has led me to a greater journey of spirituality and self-discovery. I pray it does the same for you. The hand of God is on your life.

SECTION 1

TRAVELING THROUGH THE PRAISE JOURNEY

CHAPTER 1

——○○○❖○○○——

MY PRAISE JOURNEY

After a twenty-one-day church fast at the beginning of the New Year, which was designed to create a closer spiritual relationship with God, I did feel closer to Him. However, I sensed in my spirit that something was missing. There was a nagging pull on my heart that would not allow me to be content with the fast. I heard the Holy Spirit speaking to me. He said, "You have asked God for everything you wanted on the fast, so now go for twenty-one days of thanking Him. And don't ask for anything. Just thank Him for everything."

The first time I heard it, I thought it was an awesome idea but didn't take action. I got caught up in the everyday concerns of life and forgot. However, a couple of months later, the Holy Spirit brought back to my spirit that I needed to do this time of thanksgiving. This time I took action. I talked to my family and asked if they would join me on twenty-one days of thanking God. They agreed. I started sending them daily text messages. Understanding the importance of the Word of God, I knew that the first text had to be a scripture. Realizing that I didn't know twenty-one "Thank God" scriptures, I started searching online. Originally I only found a few, but I continued to search because I was committed to keeping my word to God. I wanted to send something besides a scripture so I also sent an "I thank God" text.

On a road trip to Florida to visit our sister church, I started listening to music and discovered Kirk Franklin's Praise on SiriusXM Satellite Radio, and decided to share a Christian music video with my family. Now my daily routine was established. Each day, I sent them a praise scripture, a Christian music video, and an "I thank God" text. Not knowing what to write, I kept the "I thank God" text short and simple. As I began to have a deeper, more intimate relationship with God, the text became more encouraging. I love music, but I was not someone who listened to it on a regular basis. However, the music became an unexpected inspiration that encouraged me. It seemed like everywhere I went there was praise music lifting my spirit. At church, the praise songs ushered me to a higher level of praise. The more I praised God, the more I wanted to praise Him. This put me in a place of peace where I could listen and hear from Him. I also found myself watching Christian TV, which allowed me to learn more about who God is.

Honestly, there were days that my schedule was busy and I didn't feel like looking for scriptures or videos on the Internet—especially when I was on vacation—but I pushed past my busyness and tiredness and kept my commitment. It helped when my family commented on the daily text or sent words of encouragement. This was extremely supportive and encouraging. However, there were days when I didn't hear from anyone and felt that no one was even reading the text messages, but I knew that I still had to keep going because I wanted to be faithful to God.

God is good and has honored my faithfulness in many ways. As a result, my husband joined the praise team at our church. I also became more involved. I enjoy church more, and I am even more excited about praise and worship and the teaching of the Word of God. I even taught my young granddaughter to thank God more. Whenever I saw her, I would ask her, "What are you thankful for?" and wait for her response, which sometimes took a while. Now she is able to come up with an answer quickly, and it is always heartfelt. We also encourage her to bless her food at mealtime, which is a great way to teach children to start thanking and praising God.

A couple of months after starting my praise journey, I attended award winning business/success coach, motivational speaker, entrepreneur, and author Dr. Stacia Pierce's amazing Ultimate Success Tour in Chicago. Dr. Stacia is the CEO and founder of Lifecoach2women.com, which is an empowering website and expert coaching program that inspires women to reach their fullest potential in business and in life. While there, the Holy Spirit revealed to me that the twenty-one days of praise was a book. I never imagined that God was going to take my personal praise journey and put it into a book to encourage others to praise Him. I believe that because I was obedient, He blessed me with this book. The Holy Spirit has been the inspiration for the book and the title: *21 Days of Praise: Seeking God's Face Instead of His Hand.* I knew when I heard the title that I had to go to the next level and not just thank God for the things He has done but also had to seek His face and praise Him for who He is.

My praise journey of sending daily text messages to my family still continues to this day and will continue until the Holy Spirit releases me. This journey continues to increase my faith and bring me closer to God. It has helped me to discover a deeper relationship with Him. I feel more of His peace, love, and presence. By praising Him, my joy has increased. I am happier than I have ever been. I also feel less stressed. I used to have a habit of going over things a number of times in my mind. But since my praise journey started, I've started spending time praising God whenever I feel worried, stressed, or anxious. And it goes away as long as my focus is on Him and not on my situation.

CHAPTER 2

———∘∘∘-⟩⊗⟨-∘∘∘———

JOURNEY TO PRAISE

I invite you to go on your own twenty-one days of praise journey. I will teach, encourage, and inspire you to passionately praise God. Whether you are starting a new experience with Him, restoring your relationship with Him, or wanting to take your relationship with Him to the next level, this journey will change your life. It will be healing for your soul. Praising God will give you a more personal and intimate connection with Him. It will open your heart to Him. It will teach you to trust Him and to receive His unconditional love. You will see that He is a good, kind, and loving Father who is concerned about you. The Bible says, "We love him, because he first loved us" (1 John 4:19).

He will become the one who you can confide in. He created you to have this type of connection with Him. The spirit of God lives in you, and He wants to connect spirit to spirit.

Using the journal will create, restore, and/or enrich your relationship with God. By making Him a priority, you are committing to putting Him first. Start your day by acknowledging God first thing in the morning by saying, "Good morning, God! I love you." It will cause your day to go well and your level of praise to grow. You will discover that it is about Him and what He desires. And end your day by saying, "Good night, God! Thank you for this day." You will experience more of Him, His love, and His peace.

My desire is to help you learn to discover how to praise Him more. I heard the Holy Spirit say to ask you, "What if you were just one praise away from God blessing you with what you have been asking Him for? One praise God? One hallelujah? One glory? Would you say it? What if you were ten praises away? What if you were one hundred away? Would you praise Him?" If so, you will learn to praise God as if your breakthrough, joy, healing, and wealth were just a few praises away and see how He blesses your life.

This book is your blueprint to praise. It will introduce you to how to move from only praising Him corporately on Sunday morning to a lifestyle of continuous personal praise. You will grow from seeing God as an unattainable supernatural being who is too big and too far away for you to know Him to having a more intimate personal relationship with Him. He wants to touch your heart and fill you with His presence. He wants to trade your sadness and loneliness with joy and happiness. However, you need to spend time seeking His face to begin to live in an atmosphere of His presence. Praising Him is an awesome way to spend time with Him because it takes the attention off of you and onto Him.

My purpose for writing *21 Days of Praise* is to teach you

that there is no mystery to praising Him. It is not just for pastors or the praise-and-worship team at your church. It is also not about just being more positive and thinking positive. It is about having a loving and spiritual connection with God by speaking words of praise to Him. Since we are not embarrassed to call on God in times of trouble, we must not be embarrassed to praise Him. He is the same God who heard your cry, healed you, comforted you, answered your prayers, and provided for you when no one else could or would. He wants to speak to you and to give you peace, joy, and blessings. He wants to give you clear direction in every area of your life. He desires a closer relationship with you. The best reward is drawing closer to Him.

The Bible says, "Draw nigh to God, and he will draw nigh to you" (James 4:8).

SECTION 2
KNOWING GOD

CHAPTER 3

─o○o─⚜─o○o─

WHO IS GOD?

I am the Alpha and the Omega, the beginning
and the end, the first and the last.
—Revelation 22:13

And God said unto Moses, I AM THAT I AM.
—Exodus 3:14

In order to really praise God, you must discover who He is.
The Bible tells who and what He is. It is filled with descriptions
of His many names, including God, Father, Jehovah, and
Lord. He is described as the following:

- Creator

In the beginning God created the heaven and the earth.
—Genesis 1:1

- Spirit

> God is spirit, and they that worship him must
> worship him in spirit and in truth.
> —John 4:24

- Holy

And one cried unto another, and said, Holy, holy, holy, is
the Lord of hosts: the whole earth is full of his glory.
—Isaiah 6:3

- Love

He that loveth not knoweth not God; for God is love.
—1 John 4:8

- Good

> O taste and see that the Lord is good:
> blessed is the man that trusteth in him.
> —Psalm 34:8

- Righteous

For therein is the righteousness of God revealed from
faith to faith: as it is written, The just shall live by faith.
—Romans 1:17

- Gracious

> For by grace are ye saved through faith; and
> that not of yourselves: it is the gift of God.
> —Ephesians 2:8

- Peace

And the peace of God, which passeth all understanding,
shall keep your hearts and minds through Christ Jesus.
—Philippians 4:7

- Unchanging

> For I am the LORD, I change not.
> —Malachi 3:6

- Merciful and Faithful

It is of the LORD's mercies that we are not consumed,
because his compassions fail not. They are new
every morning: great is thy faithfulness.
—Lamentations 3:22–23

- Truthful

God is not a man, that he should lie; neither the son of
man, that he should repent: hath he said, and shall he not
do it? or hath he spoken, and shall he not make it good?
—Numbers 23:19

CHAPTER 4

———∘∘∘◗◖◗∘∘∘———

SEEKING HIS FACE

When thou saidst, Seek ye my face; my heart
said unto thee, Thy face, Lord will I seek.
—Psalm 27:8

Seek the Lord and his strength, seek his face continually.
—1 Chronicles 16:11

And ye shall seek me, and find me, when ye
shall search for me with all your heart.
—Jeremiah 29:13

Seeking God starts with making a decision to love Him with
your whole heart. The Bible says, "And thou shalt love the
Lord thy God with all thy heart, and with all thy soul, and
with all thy mind, and with all thy strength: this is the first
commandment" (Mark 12:30).

Partial or divided love for Him comes from distractions
in your life. When you make Him a priority, you offer Him

your whole heart. You will learn to seek Him by getting to know Him, loving Him, and praising Him. You give your heart to what you value the most. The Bible says, "For where your treasure is, there will your heart be also" (Matthew 6:21). This is why Satan is after your heart. He knows that what you give your heart to controls your life, so he wants to keep you away from an intimate relationship with God. This is why he tries to deceive you by filling your mind with evil, negative thoughts, and desires that only bring you harm. However, if you give your heart to God, you will have a renewed mind and a close, personal relationship with Him. Keep your mind and heart on Him. He only wants the best for you.

God wants you to seek His presence continuously. When you seek Him, you will find Him. He wants you to have a desire to pursue His presence so that He can reveal Himself to you. He is always thinking of you. Pray and ask God to help you to seek His face. He will lead and guide you, but you have to spend time with Him to hear Him. There are times when we think that we are too busy to spend time seeking His face and that we are doing good just going to church. But it's strange how we are never too busy to seek His hand for something that we want or need. We seek His hand for blessings, protection, healing, and help in times of trouble. It's like the parents whose child has grown up and they want to spend time with him or her, but the child is too busy to call or visit. However, the child seeks the parents in times of trouble or need. God wants you to spend time with Him. He loves you and wants to wipe away your tears, help conquer your fears, protect you from the storm, lead you into His

15

loving arms, heal you, and provide for you. However, He also wants you to honor and respect Him by telling Him how much you love Him and want to have a deeper connection with Him. The Bible says, "I love them that love me; and those that seek me early shall find me" (Proverbs 8:17). God has a plan for your life and needs to spend time with you to show you your purpose. To accomplish your purpose, praising Him has to become a priority. It is when you are praising Him that He has your attention and you can hear what He is saying. If you have ever wondered why you can't seem to get where you desire to be in your life or why you pray for something but don't get an answer, the answers you seek are in God. You have been taught how to pray and ask Him for whatever you want and need, but you must make a conscious effort to learn to spend even more time praising Him. Praise is what pleases Him.

21 Days of Praise will help you seek His face and have a closer relationship with Him. The more you seek Him, the more you will become more like Him. The Bible says, "So God created man in his own image, in the image of God created he him; male and female created he them" (Genesis 1:27).

But you must make the commitment and time to regularly seek Him. As you spend more time with Him, you will want to spend more with Him because there is nothing like being in His presence and there is so much He wants to reveal to you. It will take time to go to new levels of intimacy with Him. However, seeking and praising Him will help you seek more than just His hand. It will manifest a better life for you.

SECTION 3
PATH TO PURPOSEFUL PRAISE

CHAPTER 5

———∘∘∘⟡∘∘∘———

DIFFERENCE BETWEEN THANKING GOD AND PRAISING HIM

Thanking God

Enter into his gates with thanksgiving, and into his courts
with praise: be thankful unto him, and bless his name.
—Psalm 100:4

O give thanks unto the LORD; for he is
good: for his mercy endureth for ever.
—Psalm 136:1

There is a difference between thanking God and praising
Him. Thanking God is accessing His hand—His giving
nature. It is thanking Him for what He has done and
provided. God wants to bless you because He is a good and
loving God. It is important to speak words of thanksgiving
and appreciation to Him for what He does. Since He is the

one who gives everything, we owe all our thanks to Him. Take a minute to think about all the things that He has done for you. Think about how God has provided for you and helped you in times of difficult situations. Thanking Him brings more blessings, which gives you more to be grateful for. What you focus on increases.

What has God brought you through? How has He blessed you? Think on these things and thank Him for it.

Below are some suggestions of things that you could thank God for. If some of these things are not present in your life, thank Him for it now and speak it into your life. The Bible says,

> And Jesus answering saith to them, Have faith in God. For verily I say to you, That whosoever shall say to this mountain, Be thou removed, and be thou cast into the sea; and shall not doubt in his heart, but shall believe that those things which he saith shall come to pass; he shall have whatever he saith. Therefore I says unto you, What things soever ye desire, when ye pray, believe that ye receive them, and ye shall have them.
>
> —Mark 11:22–24

- waking you today
- saved you from sin
- loving others and being loved
- answered prayers

- supplying your needs
- having a sound mind
- living your authentic life
- food and shelter
- your job/career/business
- good health
- family and friends
- comfort in times of trouble, grief, and sorrow
- always being there for you
- supportive pastor and church
- clean drinking water
- military protection
- freedom to vote
- freedom to praise God
- freedom of speech
- living your best life

Thanking God is an important part of communication with Him and getting closer to Him. It prepares you for entering into praising Him. Thanking Him is like a child saying to his or her parent, "Thank you for buying me a car." However, praising is when the child says, "You are the best parents ever. I am who I am because of you. You are so kind and loving. I love you with all my heart. I want to be just like you when I grow up." Or when someone thanks his or her spouse and says, "Thank you, honey, for taking out the garbage." However, praising the spouse is saying, "Honey, you are amazing. I rush home just to spend time with you. You are the reason our family is happy and successful. You look just as beautiful as the day we married." There is a big difference between thanking and praising. God does want you to thank Him for what He does and provides, but He wants you to praise Him more for who He is. The goal is to seek His face more than His hand.

CHAPTER 6

————∘○○⧓○○∘————

PURPOSEFUL PRAISE

For the LORD is great, and greatly to be
praised; he is to be feared above all gods.
—Psalm 96:4

From the rising of the sun unto the going down
of the same the LORD's name is to be praised.
—Psalm 113:3

What Is Praising God?

We are a spirit made in God's image, which is how we
communicate with Him. We have a soul. And we live in a
physical body. Our heart's desire is to seek Him. However,
because He gives us free will, we have the ability to choose
whether we will actually praise Him. Praising Him is our
spiritual offering. It is celebrating and boasting on who He is.
It is speaking well about Him. Telling Him that you love, exalt,
respect, honor, and adore Him. It is giving Him compliments.

Think about how it feels when people say something nice about you. When people say, "You are awesome. I love you. I couldn't have made it without you. You are good and kind." Well, just like you love to hear good things about yourself, God loves to hear you say good things about Him. It is an expression of love. It is the missing piece in your life that your soul longs for.

You might be thinking that you already praise God, but I invite you to evaluate your praise time with Him. Every day you are making a decision whether or not to praise Him, whether you are conscious of it or not. There is always room for growth in pursing your relationship with Him. Going to the next level of praise will take you to the next level of peace, joy, and abundance. The more you praise Him, the more powerful you will become in every area of your life. The more you praise Him, the more He will fill you up with His presence.

Because God made you to praise Him, He gives your spirit the desire to praise Him. Praising God gives Him glory and honor. He is worthy. Praising Him reminds you of His greatness, His power, and His presence in your life. It transforms the direction of your life. As you draw closer to Him, He will draw closer to you. He loves your praise and is after your heart. Also, it will make you feel good. Furthermore, it will increase your faith and cause God to act on your behalf. You can never praise Him too much. Being in His presence is where you want to be. It is where you can be still and spend time with Him, and it is where change happens in your life. It is something that cannot be rushed. It takes a sacrifice of your time.

It is important to invest your time into praising God in order to make your relationship with Him first in your life. It is about setting your priorities in order. Everyone says that he or she is so busy, but is he or she happy? Whatever you focus on has priority in your life and shapes your future. Putting God as your first priority will help make every area of your life fall into place. When you spend time with Him, you are valuing who He is. By investing your time with Him, He will help you do more than you ever imagined. It will not only bless you but also generations to come.

If you have days when you don't feel like praising God because you are tired, it's not Sunday, or you are going through difficult times, remember you don't just praise Him when you feel like it; you praise Him even when you don't. It is a choice, a sacrifice of your will. He will not force you to praise Him. You must exercise your will and praise Him.

I remember a couple of years ago when my mother unexpectedly died. She was an active woman full of life: exercising three times a week, going to Bible study on Wednesdays, and ushering at church on Sundays. One day she wasn't feeling well so I took her to the ER. The doctors admitted her, saying that she had an infection. The next day, they said she had cancer, and within a week, she passed away. My family and I were devastated. She was the center of our lives, an amazing light of God on this earth. Although I didn't understand why this happened and went through a period of intense grief, I knew I had to trust God to get through it. What saved me was a scripture I said several times a day. "He healeth the broken in heart and bindeth up their wounds" (Psalm 147:3).

It changed everything. I knew I had to rely on God's Word, His love, and His presence. I also had to cry out to Him words of thanks because I still had a lot to be grateful for and He was still my God and my source. I learned that you can get lost in a spirit of grief and darkness and that God has to bring you out, but you have to let Him. He is our light and Savior. We must seek Him in times of trouble, and He will show us the way. Some days I could only say, "The peace of the Lord is with me," repeatedly throughout the day just to make it. Other days it was "Hallelujah" all day long. It kept my mind on Him and not on my grief. He became everything to me. I talked to Him all day about the pain of losing my mom, especially in the late-night hours when everyone was asleep. Although I still didn't understand why it happened, God was my comforter, my strength, my joy, and my peace, which I desperately needed. I never would have made it without Him. I did the things that I am sharing with you. I praised God even when it was difficult, which is how I know it works. Even now, whenever the spirit of grief, guilt, loneliness, stress, and worry tries to come upon me, I just start praising and thanking God and telling Him how wonderful He is, how much I love Him, and how He brought me through difficult times.

Having a relationship with God is personal. No one can take the journey for you. You have to walk it. But there is no need to fear. He is your creator and He loves you. He only wants the best for you. Think of the people you love. You only want the best for them. Let Him love you. The fact that God wants to spend time with you should help you understand how important you are to Him. The Bible says,

> What is man, that thou art mindful of him? and the son of man, that thou visitest him? For thou hast made him a little lower than the angels, and hast crowned him with glory and honour. Thou madest him to have dominion over the works of thy hands; thou hast put all things under his feet.
>
> —Psalm 8:4–6

Step out of your comfort zone and start praising Him. Ask Him to help you know how to praise Him. Be honest with Him about how you are feeling. You can talk to Him about anything, even about praising Him. He will touch your heart and your spirit will praise Him. Wait on Him, and trust Him to minister to your spirit. Praising Him when it's challenging will increase your faith and help you through difficult times. An attitude of praise will teach you how to be full of joy. The more you praise Him, the more things will improve.

Benefits of Praising God

One of the greatest benefits of praising God is that it pleases Him. It manifests His power and causes Him to inhabit the praises of His people. It reminds you that He is your source and that He is in control, which takes the pressure off you to be in control. It will also relieve stress, calm you, and put you in a positive state of mind. Praising Him reminds you of His power and greatness. It brings you closer to Him. It takes your mind off of your problems and onto Him. It is an example to others of God's greatness, peace, and joy. Furthermore, it releases His giving and miracles. Good things begin to happen when you praise Him. There is nothing impossible for Him, so be prepared for all of the good that He will do in your life as a result of you praising Him. Your future will be greater than your past because you are living a lifestyle of continuously praising God. Expect miracles!

Praising Him keeps you speaking positive words instead of negative ones of doubt, fear, and unbelief. Your mind cannot hold both a negative thought and a positive one at the same time, so which one will you choose? Start praising God and see how it changes your attitude and your emotions. The thoughts you choose to feed are the ones that dominate, so choose to feed thoughts of praise. Finally, praising God gives us a powerful tool against Satan. Satan will not stay around to hear you praise God, so praising God in times of trouble is a powerful spiritual weapon against Satan. He will leave but when he tries to come after you again, remember that praising God makes him leave.

How to Praise God

Jesus is our example of how to praise God. He taught us how to praise and honor God when He taught the Lord's Prayer.

Our Father which art in heaven, Hallowed be thy name.
For thine is the kingdom, and the power,
and the glory, for ever. Amen.
—Matthew 6:9 & 13

There are several ways to praise God, and using Jesus' example of praising Him at the beginning and end of your prayers is an excellent way to do it. You can praise Him with your mind, body, and soul. You can praise God with your mind by thinking about Him. Reading the Bible is a great way to think about Him and learn how He thinks. Take time to get the clutter out of your head; close your eyes and meditate on Him. The more you focus on thinking about Him, the more you will want to focus on praising Him. The more you praise Him, the higher your level of spiritual experience with God.

You can praise Him with your body by using your mouth to speak or sing words of adoration to Him. It can be a sweet sound of a whisper, a heartfelt cry, or a loud shout. It is good to speak your words of praise. Would you rather have people think how much they love you and how important you are to them or have them say it out loud to you? God wants to hear you say it out loud too. The more you praise out loud, the more you will be able to do it. The power is in the doing. You can also praise Him by saying or singing one word or phrase repeatedly throughout the day, like "Hallelujah," "Glory," or "You are my source." You could even use the same word or phrase throughout your praise journey. Praising God is more about your spirit praising Him than the exact words you say as long as they are words of praise. You can praise Him through songs and music. You can also praise God with your body by dancing, jumping for joy, stomping your feet, clapping or lifting your hands, bowing down before Him in reverence for who He is, kneeling down, lying flat before Him, or playing an instrument. The desire is to praise Him. You decide how you want to do it.

You can praise God with your soul by giving Him your passionate devotion and living a life that is pleasing to Him. The Bible says, "And thou shalt love the Lord thy God with all thy heart, and with all thy soul, and with all thy mind, and with all thy strength; this is the first commandment" (Mark 12:30).

God will teach you how to praise Him and what He wants to hear so that your praise will be pleasing to Him. Praise is something that your spirit knows how to do and wants to do. Sometimes you will think words of praise or write them, and sometimes you will open your mouth and praise Him.

You can praise Him anywhere. You can praise Him in church. You can praise Him at work during your lunch hour or when you are having a challenging time at work. Praise Him in your car on your drive to and from work. Praise Him at home in a quiet and special place where you can be in silence in His presence, waiting to hear what He wants to say to you, or when you are doing daily tasks. The when and where are not as important as why you are praising Him. Just do it.

You can praise God anytime. Praising Him should not be limited to only on Sunday. Praise Him every day. Praise Him when you are happy, confused, sad, angry, worried, or scared. It will take your mind off your emotions and difficult times and onto God, who can change any situation. I am a witness that even when you are going through challenging times, your spirit will want to praise Him. I know that if I praise Him, my mind will shift from thinking about my problems to thinking about praising and pleasing Him. If I lift Him up, I know that He will lift me up. And you don't have to praise Him for long periods of time for your mind to shift to Him. Over time you just develop the habit of praising Him. You will run to praising Him in times of trouble because you know that He is your Savior. So find ways to incorporate praise into your daily life. I put notes that say, "Praise God!" around the house (on the refrigerator and the bathroom mirror) to remind me to praise Him. And sending the daily praise scripture, Christian song, and "I thank God" text messages helps to keep me on track praising God.

Find something that works for you and that you will enjoy offering to God.

Here are some of God's attributes and characteristics with words of praise to help you praise Him:

- Hallelujah (the highest praise).
- Glory and honor to God.

- Bless the name of the Lord.
- Praise God.
- Praise the Lord.
- I exalt you.
- El Elyon. (You are the Most High God.)
- El Shaddai. (You are Lord God Almighty.)
- Jehovah Adon. (You are Lord of lords.)
- Jehovah Jireh. (You are the Lord who provides.)
- Jehovah Nissi. (You are the Lord my banner.)
- Jehovah Raah. (You are the Lord my shepherd.)
- Jehovah Rapha. (You are the Lord who heals.)
- Jehovah Shalom. (You are the Lord my peace.)
- Jehovah Shammah. (You are the Lord who is present.)
- Jehovah Tsidkenu. (You are the Lord my righteousness.)
- You are the King of glory.
- You are King of kings.
- You are my creator.
- You are a loving God.
- You are the God of comfort.
- You are the Holy One.
- You are a good God.
- You are Lord of my life.
- You are a giving God.
- You are the God who answers my prayer.
- You are the God of miracles.
- You are a merciful God.
- You are a faithful God.
- You are a forgiving God.

CHAPTER 7

———∘οο⧓οο∘———

WRITING YOUR WAY TO PRAISING GOD

And the LORD answered me, and said, Write the vision, and
make it plain upon tables, that he may run that readeth it.
—Habakkuk 2:2

What Is Journaling?

Journaling is writing down your thoughts, desires, questions,
reflections, ideas, experiences, and life events. It is a place
to record what God says to you, what He has done for you,
and what you want to say to Him. It can be as simple as using
a notebook or this praise journal, which is designed to help
you praise God purposefully. Words have power, whether
spoken or written, which is why it is important to do both.
Your spirit responds to what you write and knows when you
are speaking and writing from your heart. Journaling will

help you write down your praises and thanks, and spend time with God. You just have to do it. Listen to what God is saying, receive it, and write it down.

Journaling will help you open up your heart and receive what God wants to share with you. It will teach you to seek His face and not always His hand. It will help you see the progress of your praise and time with God. To have a personal relationship with Him, you must spend time with Him. Like any other relationship, it will take intentional action on your part. Journaling will help you write your way to a deeper connection with God. It's your personal journal, so write openly and honestly to Him. This is how you will receive the greatest rewards. What you write will get into your spirit and cause you to have to a deeper, more intimate relationship with Him. He just wants you to spend time with Him. He wants you to speak to Him from your heart with words of love, adoration, honor, and glory. As you spend time with Him, you will become more comfortable praising Him. The more detail you write in your journal, the closer relationship you will have with God.

How to Journal

Don't worry if you don't know what to say to Him or what to write. Just write. Don't worry about writing perfectly, spelling, grammar, or editing. It's your journal; no one else will read it. When you try to write perfectly, you miss the authenticity that comes from just letting your thoughts flow.

Also, don't be afraid to ask God questions when you journal. You can't get answers if you never ask questions.

Journaling can be done anytime and anywhere. It can be done in a quiet space of your home or at your desk at work. It can be done while waiting in the car or waiting for an appointment. Give God the best parts of your day. You can spend the beginning and/or end of your day praising Him. How awesome it is to start your day full of energy by praising God. Or end your day in a spirit of peace with Him. Journaling will only take a few minutes a day. Your creator who protects you throughout the day and loves you more than anyone else ever could, is worth a few minutes a day.

SECTION 4
PRAISE JOURNAL

CHAPTER 8

—ooo—✦—ooo—

DAILY COMPONENTS OF YOUR PRAISE JOURNAL

Daily Scripture

> This book of the law shall not depart out of thy mouth,
> but thou shall meditate therein day and night, that
> thou mayest observe to do according to all that is
> written therein; for then thou shalt make thy way
> prosperous, and then thou shalt have good success.
> —Joshua 1:8

Every day you will start with a key scripture from the Bible. It is your foundation to knowing God. It will show you how He thinks and give you the answers you seek. The Bible says to mediate on the scriptures day and night to know God and to grow in Him and live your best life. It is helpful to read your daily scripture a few times throughout the day to get it in your spirit. It is also helpful to read it out loud. It is good for you to hear yourself read God's Word. Meditate on it. Write it down. Make it part of your day and apply it to your life. When reading scriptures, you can make it more personal by inserting your name in the scriptures. This will produce an even deeper relationship with God.

What Is God Saying to me?

> I will hear what God the LORD will speak.
> —Psalm 85:8

Pray and ask God questions. You can ask Him what the key scripture means, about your life's purpose, what He wants you to do about your problems, and what He wants to say to you. The questions are endless. Then listen for Him to answer and write it down. Listen quietly for what He is saying. Don't rush to write down an answer. It will be a still small voice that speaks to your heart. It will be God's spirit that speaks to your spirit. Write down what He says because you might not remember it later and He might not repeat it. Learning to hear from God will change your life. This is how you develop a personal relationship with Him. Whatever He tells you to do, know that He has equipped you to do it. Trust Him as He guides you beyond the life that you imagined. He has created an amazing purpose for you. Listen for Him to tell you not only your purpose but also how to accomplish it.

God, I Thank You for

> In every thing give thanks: for this is the will
> of God in Christ Jesus concerning you.
> —1 Thessalonians 5:18

You want to thank God because He is good and loves to give His children good gifts, and wants to bless you with the desires of your heart. Thankfulness not only pleases Him; it is good for your spirit. Once you start, you will find that the more thankful you are, the more blessings you will receive and the happier you will become. It will help you focus on the positive things in life. This section is provided so that you can write down what He has done, is doing, and will do for you and those you love. You can refer back to the "Thanking God" section (Chapter 5) for suggestions on things to write. Thanking Him is also a great way to prepare for praising Him.

God, I Praise You Because You Are

> Because thy lovingkindness is better than
> life, my lips shall praise thee.
> —Psalm 63:3

Praising Him for who He is instead of what He does for you causes you to shower Him with words of adoration, reverence, and respect. He loves praises and created you to praise Him. This section is provided so that you can write down your words of praise to Him. He just wants you to be authentic and to praise Him with your whole heart. He longs to hear what you have to say. You can refer back to the "Purposeful Praise" section (Chapter 6) for suggestions on what to write.

SECTION 5
LET THE JOURNEY BEGIN!

CHAPTER 9

———◦◦◦◦◦◦———

YOUR NEXT TWENTY-ONE DAYS

For the next twenty-one days, you will develop the habit of praising God. A habit is practicing or doing something in a repetitive manner until it becomes a way of life. Experts say it takes twenty-one days to form a habit. *21 Days of Praise* is designed to inspire a life-long change in your heart toward praising God. It all starts with the discipline of spending time with Him. To accomplish the purpose that He has for you, praising Him has to become a habit.

The next twenty-one days create a new beginning that will transform your life. God wants to take you to new heights in Him and new heights of success. All you have to do is step out of your comfort zone and commit to this new experience to take full advantage of what He has for you. Although it can be easy to get distracted by everyday issues of life, stay focused and committed to spending time with God.

He wants you to glorify Him, to get you to know Him better, and to prepare you for your purpose. When you praise Him, He has your attention, heart, mind, and soul. You are fully His. He can speak to you, and you can listen free from distractions.

My Prayer for You

Father,

I am thankful for all that you have done. Lord God you are worthy of all the praise. Blessed is your holy name. I pray in Jesus' name that you speak to the hearts of those who are going on this praise journey so that they will know your voice and how much you love them. Lord God, open their hearts so that they can hear everything that you want to say to them, and help them to receive it. Father, help them to have a more intimate and more personal relationship with you, and to develop a lifelong commitment to purposeful praise. Bless them with a long life of joy, health, peace, and happiness. Lord God, I pray that at the end of the twenty-one-day journey, they will be forever changed and share the power of praise.

Amen.

I am excited for you because I know that great things are going to happen for you. It happened to me and I am forever changed. Now all you have to do is commit to this

journey for the next twenty-one days by setting aside time for
God. He is worthy of these few moments of your time. He is
waiting on you, and He will bless you for it. He wants to do
something special in your life. You can trust Him. You have
tried everything else; now try praising Him. Make your time
with God a priority. You will never be the same.

Prayer of Salvation and Rededication

If you have never accepted Jesus Christ as your personal
Savior or you want to rededicate your life to Christ, the Bible
says, "That if thou shalt confess with thy mouth the Lord
Jesus, and shalt believe in thine heart that God hath raised
him from the dead, thou shalt be saved" (Romans 10:9).

Salvation is not about religion. It is about a relationship
with God through His Son Jesus Christ. The Bible also says,
"Jesus saith unto him, I am the way, the truth, and the life;
no man cometh unto the Father, but by me" (John 14:6).

If you think that you are not worthy of a relationship with
God or reconnecting with Him because of all of the things
that you have done, the Bible teaches, "For all have sinned,
and come short of the glory of God" (Romans 3:23).

Let go of your past. God is good and wants to change
the direction of your life. He loves you and wants to have
an intimate relationship with you. Let Him come into your
heart. Pray this simple prayer:

Lord,

I admit that I am a sinner and ask for your forgiveness. I believe in my heart that you died on the cross for my sins and that God raised you from the dead. Come into my life. I confess that you are my Lord and Savior.

Thank you, Lord Jesus.

If you prayed this prayer, you are a child of God and you have changed the direction of your life forever. God has a great plan for your destiny. Stay connected to Him and He will take you places you never imagined. I know because it is the most important prayer I ever prayed and the best decision I have ever made.

Don't ever settle for less than God's best for your life. Live by faith that what He says is true. Now lets begin your journey!

SECTION 6

TWENTY-ONE DAYS OF PRAISE JOURNAL

Day 1

Scripture

Let every thing that hath breath praise
the LORD. Praise ye the Lord.
—Psalm 150:6

What is God saying to me?

_____

_____

_____

_____

_____

_____

_____

_____

_____

_____

_____

_____

_____

_____

_____

God, I thank You for

_____

_____

_____

_____

_____

_____

_____

_____

God, I praise You because You are

_____

_____

_____

_____

_____

_____

_____

_____

_____

Day 2

Scripture

I will bless the LORD at all times: his praise
shall continually be in my mouth.

—Psalm 34:1

What is God saying to me?

_____

_____

_____

_____

_____

_____

_____

_____

_____

_____

_____

_____

_____

_____

God, I thank You for

_____

_____

_____

_____

_____

_____

_____

_____

God, I praise You because You are

_____

_____

_____

_____

_____

_____

_____

_____

_____

_____

Day 3

Scripture

Rejoice in the Lord always: and again I say, Rejoice.

—Philippians 4:4

What is God saying to me?

_____

_____

_____

_____

_____

_____

_____

_____

_____

_____

_____

_____

_____

_____

_____

_____

God, I thank You for

_____

_____

_____

_____

_____

_____

_____

_____

God, I praise You because You are

_____

_____

_____

_____

_____

_____

_____

_____

_____

_____

Day 4

Scripture

In God will I praise his word: in the
LORD will I praise his word.

—PSALM 56:10

What is God saying to me?

_____

_____

_____

_____

_____

_____

_____

_____

_____

_____

_____

_____

_____

_____

_____

_____

_____

God, I thank You for

_____

_____

_____

_____

_____

_____

_____

God, I praise You because You are

_____

_____

_____

_____

_____

_____

_____

_____

_____

_____

Day 5

Scripture

It is a good thing to give thanks unto the LORD, and to sing praises unto thy name, O Most High.

—Psalm 92:1

What is God saying to me?

_____

_____

_____

_____

_____

_____

_____

_____

_____

_____

_____

_____

_____

_____

_____

_____

God, I thank You for

_____

_____

_____

_____

_____

_____

_____

_____

God, I praise You because You are

_____

_____

_____

_____

_____

_____

_____

_____

_____

_____

_____

Day 6

Scripture

> I will praise thee; for I am fearfully and
> wonderfully made: marvellous are thy works;
> and that my soul knoweth right well.
> —Psalm 139:14

What is God saying to me?

_____

_____

_____

_____

_____

_____

_____

_____

_____

_____

_____

_____

_____

_____

God, I thank You for

_____

_____

_____

_____

_____

_____

_____

_____

God, I praise You because You are

_____

_____

_____

_____

_____

_____

_____

_____

_____

_____

Day 7

Scripture

> Every day will I bless thee; and I will
> praise thy name for ever and ever.
> —Psalm 145:2

What is God saying to me?

_____

_____

_____

_____

_____

_____

_____

_____

_____

_____

_____

_____

_____

_____

_____

_____

God, I thank You for

_____

_____

_____

_____

_____

_____

_____

_____

God, I praise You because You are

_____

_____

_____

_____

_____

_____

_____

_____

_____

_____

Day 8

Scripture

Oh that men would praise the LORD for his goodness,
and for his wonderful works to the children of men!

—Psalm 107:8

What is God saying to me?

_____

_____

_____

_____

_____

_____

_____

_____

_____

_____

_____

_____

_____

_____

_____

God, I thank You for

_____

_____

_____

_____

_____

_____

_____

_____

God, I praise You because You are

_____

_____

_____

_____

_____

_____

_____

_____

_____

_____

_____

Day 9

Scripture

By him therefore let us offer the sacrifice of
praise to God continually, that is, the fruit
of our lips giving thanks to his name.

—Hebrews 13:15

What is God saying to me?

_____

_____

_____

_____

_____

_____

_____

_____

_____

_____

_____

_____

God, I thank You for

_____

_____

_____

_____

_____

_____

_____

God, I praise You because You are

_____

_____

_____

_____

_____

_____

_____

_____

_____

Day 10

Scripture

Thou art my God, and I will praise thee:
thou art my God, I will exalt thee.

—Psalm 118:28

What is God saying to me?

_____

_____

_____

_____

_____

_____

_____

_____

_____

_____

_____

_____

_____

_____

God, I thank You for

_____

_____

_____

_____

_____

_____

_____

_____

God, I praise You because You are

_____

_____

_____

_____

_____

_____

_____

_____

_____

_____

_____

Day 11

Scripture

From the rising of the sun unto the going down of the same the LORD's name is to be praised.

—Psalm 113:3

What is God saying to me?

_____

_____

_____

_____

_____

_____

_____

_____

_____

_____

_____

_____

_____

_____

_____

God, I thank You for

_____

_____

_____

_____

_____

_____

_____

_____

God, I praise You because You are

_____

_____

_____

_____

_____

_____

_____

_____

_____

_____

_____

Day 12

Scripture

I will praise thee, O Lord, with my whole heart;
I will shew forth all thy marvellous works.

—Psalm 9:1

What is God saying to me?

_____

_____

_____

_____

_____

_____

_____

_____

_____

_____

_____

_____

_____

_____

God, I thank You for

_____

_____

_____

_____

_____

_____

_____

_____

God, I praise You because You are

_____

_____

_____

_____

_____

_____

_____

_____

_____

_____

_____

Day 13

Scripture

I will declare thy name unto my brethren: in the midst of the congregation will I praise thee.

—Psalm 22:22

What is God saying to me?

_____

_____

_____

_____

_____

_____

_____

_____

_____

_____

_____

_____

_____

_____

God, I thank You for

_____

_____

_____

_____

_____

_____

_____

_____

God, I praise You because You are

_____

_____

_____

_____

_____

_____

_____

_____

_____

_____

_____

Day 14

Scripture

> For the LORD is great, and greatly to be
> praised: he is to be feared above all gods.
> —Psalm 96:4

What is God saying to me?

_____

_____

_____

_____

_____

_____

_____

_____

_____

_____

_____

_____

God, I thank You for

_____

_____

_____

_____

_____

_____

_____

_____

God, I praise You because You are

_____

_____

_____

_____

_____

_____

_____

_____

_____

_____

_____

Day 15

Scripture

I will sing unto the LORD as long as I live: I will sing praise to my God while I have my being.

—Psalm 104:33

What is God saying to me?

_____

_____

_____

_____

_____

_____

_____

_____

_____

_____

_____

_____

God, I thank You for

_____

_____

_____

_____

_____

_____

_____

God, I praise You because You are

_____

_____

_____

_____

_____

_____

_____

_____

_____

_____

Day 16

Scripture

Blessed be the name of the LORD from
this time forth and for evermore.
—Psalm 113:2

What is God saying to me?

_____

_____

_____

_____

_____

_____

_____

_____

_____

_____

_____

_____

_____

_____

_____

God, I thank You for

_____

_____

_____

_____

_____

_____

_____

_____

God, I praise You because You are

_____

_____

_____

_____

_____

_____

_____

_____

_____

_____

Day 17

Scripture

Let my mouth be filled with thy praise
and with thy honour all the day.

—Psalm 71:8

What is God saying to me?

God, I thank You for

_____

_____

_____

_____

_____

_____

_____

God, I praise You because You are

_____

_____

_____

_____

_____

_____

_____

_____

_____

Day 18

Scripture

Be thou exalted, O God, above the heavens:
and thy glory above all the earth.
—Psalm 108:5

What is God saying to me?

_____

_____

_____

_____

_____

_____

_____

_____

_____

_____

_____

_____

_____

_____

God, I thank You for

_____

_____

_____

_____

_____

_____

_____

_____

_____

God, I praise You because You are

_____

_____

_____

_____

_____

_____

_____

_____

_____

_____

_____

Day 19

Scripture

> Bless the LORD, O my soul: and all that
> is within me, bless his holy name.
> —Psalm 103:1

What is God saying to me?

_____

_____

_____

_____

_____

_____

_____

_____

_____

_____

_____

_____

_____

_____

_____

_____

God, I thank You for

_____

_____

_____

_____

_____

_____

_____

_____

God, I praise You because You are

_____

_____

_____

_____

_____

_____

_____

_____

_____

_____

_____

_____

Day 20

Scripture

I will praise thee, O LORD my God, with all my
heart: and I will glorify thy name for evermore.

—Psalm 86:12

What is God saying to me?

_____

_____

_____

_____

_____

_____

_____

_____

_____

_____

_____

_____

_____

_____

_____

God, I thank You for

_____

_____

_____

_____

_____

_____

_____

_____

God, I praise You because You are

_____

_____

_____

_____

_____

_____

_____

_____

_____

_____

Day 21

Scripture

Make a joyful noise unto the Lord, all ye lands. Serve the Lord with gladness: come before his presence with singing.
—Psalm 100:1–2

What is God saying to me?

_____

_____

_____

_____

_____

_____

_____

_____

_____

_____

_____

_____

_____

God, I thank You for

_____

_____

_____

_____

_____

_____

_____

_____

_____

God, I praise You because You are

_____

_____

_____

_____

_____

_____

_____

_____

_____

_____

_____

_____

CHAPTER 10

—○○○❦○○○—

NOW WHAT?

Congratulations! You just completed your praise journey! Now what? Continue to praise God. Praising Him is now a habit. You have all of the tools you need to continue this journey and to encourage others to praise God. Remember to do the things that you learned by simply reading scriptures, praising Him, and writing in your praise journal. Also, remember the goal is to praise Him more for who He is than what He does, and seek His face more than His hand. The Bible says, "But continue thou in the things which thou hast learned and hast been assured of, knowing of whom thou has learned them" (2 Timothy 3:14).

Continuing to do this will lead to a lifetime of a closer personal relationship with God. It will take you to new levels of purpose, joy, fulfillment, happiness, and much more. It's amazing what changes God can make in your life in a short period of time. Here are some things that will help you continue to seek Him, have an intimate connection with Him, continuously praise Him, and help move you toward the life He has for you:

- Read your Bible daily. It teaches you to meditate on the Word of God day and night. It is your daily spiritual food and will feed your soul. Even if you read just one scripture a day, it will impact your life. Many people read the King James Version; however, there are many versions available to help you understand the scriptures. Also, there are Bible apps, CDs, MP3s, and other devices to make the scriptures convenient and accessible.

- Pray daily. It is just talking to God. You don't need any special words. He knows you and knows how you talk, so just talk to Him.

- Praise God daily. Use the skills you learned on your praise journey to keep praising Him.

- Find a Bible-based church to grow and fellowship with other believers, and get involved.

- Listen to Christian music. I listen to SiriusXM radio's Kirk Franklin's Praise (Channel 64) and The Message (Channel 63), and Christian Broadcasting Network's (CBN) Christian radio. Watch Christian TV (Daystar, Impact Television Network, TBN, The Word Network, and CBN (*The 700 club*) are some of the networks and programs that I regularly watch), and read Christian books and magazines to grow in God and be encouraged. It will help keep you in a spirit of praise.

- Share your experience with others and who God is to you. Keep it simple and just tell what God has done for you.

CHAPTER 11

——∘o○-)⊱◈⊰(-○o∘——

HOW TO START A PRAISE GROUP

Now that you are inspired by the change you see in yourself and want to share the power of praise, you can start a support group to help encourage others to praise God. There are people waiting for you to share your story. You could be the next voice to save someone's life. Be the light in a dark world. The Bible says,

> Ye are the light of the world. A city that is set on a hill cannot be hid. Neither do men light a candle, and put it under a bushel, but on a candlestick, and it giveth light unto all that are in the house. Let your light so shine before men, that they may see your good works, and glorify your Father which is in heaven.
> —Matthew 5:14–16

Your group can be any size you choose. It can be with your spouse, family, friends, church, or youth ministry. It can be done in person, by text or phone, through social media, or by using videos. It's important for the group to pray for one another and be patient with each other because you never know what challenges the members are experiencing. The group is a powerful, supportive, and encouraging environment for teaching people the power of praising God. You want to always strive to help people feel comfortable. Remember there are no strict rules to praising Him. The goal is for everyone to grow through praising and fellowship. Enjoy the journey with others.

Sharing Your Praise Experience and Stay Connected

I would love to hear about your journey, what God has done for you, and how *21 Days of Praise* has changed your life and the lives of others. Please take a few moments to connect with me on social media and share your praise experience, and visit my website at www.LucilleWillis.com.

My desire is to ignite a praise revolution around the world.

Join the revolution. #21daysofpraise

Notes

Notes

Notes

Notes

Printed in the United States
By Bookmasters